D0845557

SUPERSTARS
of
PRO
FOOTBALL

CHAMP BAILEY

D. C. Snow

Mason Crest Publishers

Produced by OTTN Publishing in association with
21st Century Publishing and Communications, Inc.

MASON CREST PUBLISHERS INC.
370 Reed Road
Broomall, Pennsylvania 19008
(866) MCP-BOOK (toll free)
www.masoncrest.com

Printed in the United States of America.

First Printing

9 8 7 6 5 4 3 2 1

Library of Congress Cataloging-in-Publication Data

Snow, D. C.
    Champ Bailey / D.C. Snow.
        p. cm. — (Superstars of pro football)
    Includes bibliographical references.
    ISBN 978-1-4222-0544-0 (hardcover) — ISBN 978-1-4222-0819-9 (pbk.)
    1. Bailey, Champ, 1978–   —Juvenile literature. 2. Football players—Biography—
Juvenile literature. I. Title.
    GV939.B344S66 2008
    796.332092—dc22
    [B]   2008024181

Publisher's note:
All quotations in this book come from original sources, and contain the spelling
and grammatical inconsistencies of the original text.

◄◄ CROSS-CURRENTS ►►

In the ebb and flow of the currents of life we are each influenced
by many people, places, and events that we directly experience or
have learned about. Throughout the chapters of this book you will
come across **CROSS-CURRENTS** reference bubbles. These bubbles
direct you to a **CROSS-CURRENTS** section in the back of the
book that contains fascinating and informative sidebars
and related pictures. Go on. ►►

◄◄CONTENTS►►

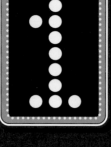

THE BEST IN THE BUSINESS

January 14, 2006, was a cool day at the Denver Broncos' football stadium. On the field, however, things were starting to heat up. The Broncos were hosting one of the league's toughest teams in a playoff game. The New England Patriots were the defending Super Bowl champions, and they were just five yards away from the Broncos' end zone.

Late in the third quarter, Denver held a 10–6 lead, but the Patriots were driving for a go-ahead score. From the Broncos' five-yard line, Patriots **quarterback** Tom Brady threw the ball in the direction of receiver Troy Brown. That was when Denver's star **cornerback**, Champ Bailey, made a huge play. Champ **intercepted** the pass, then ran toward the Patriots' goal line with the ball.

Denver Broncos cornerback Champ Bailey runs with the ball after an interception. Many football experts consider Champ the best cornerback in the National Football League today. He has picked off more than 40 passes during his career.

Champ turned on his speed and raced past the Patriots' defenders. He ran almost the entire length of the field. Champ was one yard away from a **touchdown** when Patriots tight end Ben Watson tackled him.

CROSS-CURRENTS

Read "America's Most Popular Sport" to find out more about the number of people who are football fans. Go to page 46. ▶▶

Although the Patriots had prevented Champ from scoring, his big play gave the Broncos firm control of the game. From the Patriots' one-yard line, Broncos running back Mike Anderson scored to put Denver ahead, 17–6. New England would never seriously threaten to take the lead for the rest of the game. The Broncos went on to win by a score of 27 to 13. This was Denver's first playoff victory since 1999.

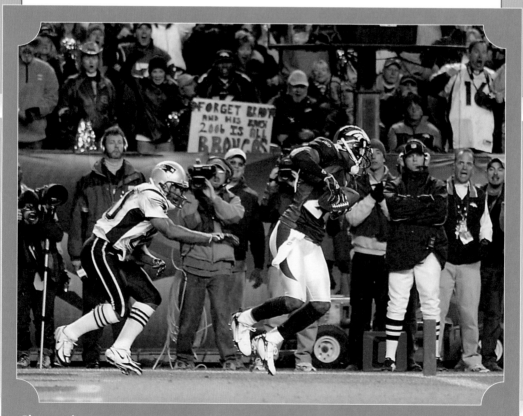

Champ intercepts a pass in the end zone during a playoff game against the New England Patriots, January 14, 2006. Champ returned the ball 101 yards, nearly scoring a touchdown.

After the game, Broncos coach Mike Shanahan gave Champ the game ball—a sign that the coach recognized the importance of Champ's 101-yard interception return. Champ's teammates also praised the cornerback. Broncos safety John Lynch said,

> **"Big-time players make big-time plays. Champ's that kind of player. When it's important, you want players like him around you. Some guys perform at the critical situations in games. He's one of those guys."**

Champ admitted that he always thinks about making such game-changing plays. During the playoff game, Champ said, he saw his opponent make a mistake. Champ was ready to take advantage:

> **"[Quarterback Tom Brady] gave me the opportunity to make a play. You've got to jump on those opportunities. That's one of the things about Brady, he's not going to throw it up there a lot for you to pick it, so you'd better jump on it while you can."**

Top Cornerback

Many people think Champ Bailey is the best cover cornerback in the National Football League (NFL). During the 2006 NFL season, Champ had what might have been the best all-around season ever by a cornerback. He had 10 interceptions, and ran one back 70 yards for a touchdown.

In addition to preventing pass plays, Champ also works to stop opponents' running plays. When a running back gets through the line of scrimmage, Champ must sometimes make the tackle. On the Broncos, Champ is almost always among the team's top tacklers each game. In 2006, Champ had 74 solo tackles and assisted on 12 other stops.

Even though the Broncos did not have a good season in 2007, Champ continued to play well. He was chosen to play in the **Pro Bowl** for the eighth time in a row. This streak of Pro Bowl selections is

CROSS-CURRENTS

To learn more about the skills that help a cornerback excel in the NFL, read "Great Cornerbacks." Go to page 47. ▶▶

Leaping high in the air, Champ grabs a pass during a 2006 game against the Pittsburgh Steelers. Champ's blazing speed, quick reflexes, and good hands make him an opposing quarterback's worst enemy.

currently the longest among defensive players. It is only four seasons shorter than the NFL's all-time record.

Great Qualities

A cornerback's most important job is to prevent the opposing team's **wide receivers** from catching passes. Champ has three qualities that make him a great cornerback. First, he is very fast. Champ can run the 40-yard dash as fast as almost any receiver he has to guard. His speed allows him to keep up with receivers as they run complex plays, and to catch up with them when they make sudden moves. In an article about Champ that appeared in *USA Today*, Oakland Raiders defensive back DeAngelo Hall explained how Champ uses his speed and his reflexes to keep wide receivers from catching passes:

> **"**[Champ is] just cat-quick. He can press receivers. He doesn't even really have to get his hands on them. He is so quick with his feet. He can break off with the receiver. A lot of corners can't get out of their **breaks**, and that's how receivers get the **curls** and **out routes**. A corner who is quick on his feet and takes them coming out of a break is going to shut them down.**"**

Second, Champ is smart and works hard before games. He studies the receivers and quarterbacks on opposing teams to learn their pass routes and strategies. The more he knows about his opponents, the better he can play defense. Before each play, Champ positions his head, hips, and feet to give himself the best chance to reach the ball before the receiver. Before a pass is thrown, Champ watches the quarterback's eyes and watches the receiver, trying to get a sense of where the ball is going to be thrown. If Champ reads the play correctly, he can get there first and intercept the pass.

The third quality that makes Champ a great cornerback is his attitude. Champ has said that he believes it is his job to catch the pass himself and go on the offense for his team. With his aggressive style of play and his sharp instincts, Champ is always working to help his team win the game.

A STAR
IS BORN

On June 22, 1978, Roland Bailey Jr. was born to Elaine and Roland Bailey Sr. The newborn had an older brother, Ronald, and an older sister Danielle. The Bailey family lived in Folkston, Georgia, a small town of about 2,200 people that is located about 45 miles from Jacksonville, Florida.

Roland Bailey Sr. had been an outstanding high school football player, but his football days had ended with a neck injury. Ronald Bailey was also a talented athlete. However, it was Roland Jr. whom Elaine nicknamed "Champ." In an interview with Mike Klis of the *Denver Post*, Elaine explained the origin of her son's nickname:

"[Champ] was so active as a child. He would never take his time and just walk. He always had a little run in him. And when he would play in the house, he liked to jump over my couch. And one day I said, 'That's going to be my little Champ.'"

Sixteen months after Champ was born, Roland Sr. and Elaine had another son, whom they named Rodney. Elaine nicknamed Champ's younger brother "Boss," after her favorite uncle.

Champ inherited his athletic ability from his parents. His dad, Roland Bailey Sr., had been offered a college football scholarship, and his mom, Elaine Bailey, once described herself as "the neighborhood girl athlete."

Champ Shows Early Promise

Even when Champ was young, many people could see that he was a good athlete. As a teenager, he played several sports for the Charlton County High School Indians. On the football team, he became the Indians' quarterback and **free safety**. Champ also competed on the track team, winning the Georgia state high jump championship in his junior year. With his jumping ability, it did not surprise many people that Champ also dunked the basketball regularly as a member of the Indians' basketball team.

CROSS-CURRENTS

To learn about the nicknames used by some other professional football players, read "NFL Nicknames." Go to page 48. ▶▶

In the fall of 1995, his senior year in high school, Champ's football coach moved him from quarterback to **tailback**. As a tailback, Champ rushed for 1,858 yards and scored 28 touchdowns. He led the Charlton County High School Indians to an 11–1 record.

Difficult Times

Champ's success in sports was very important during his early years. It gave him something to which he dedicated himself as he went through some difficult times. Several events occurred during Champ's teen years that had long-term effects on him. First, Champ's parents separated. Elaine was given custody of the children. She had to work two jobs to make ends meet.

Then, when he was only 14 years old, Champ fathered his first child. Being a father at such a young age put a great deal of pressure on Champ. He did not want to ignore his responsibilities, so Champ worked at a number of jobs while he was in high school so he could help support his child. His jobs included mowing grass and pulling weeds for the town of Folkston, working at a Dairy Queen, and working at a paper company. In an interview with Frank Schwab of the *Colorado Springs Gazette*, Champ described how being a very young father affected him:

❝I tried to take care of that, as much as I could, on my own, and leave [my parents] out of it. . . . Just trying to grow up a lot faster than I should have. It was nerve-wracking. It was tough. . . . It wasn't good for me to have a child that early, but at the same time, it made me grow up.❞

Champ grew up in Folkston, a small town of about 2,200 residents in southern Georgia. He attended Charlton County High School, where he starred as a member of the football, basketball, and track teams.

Four years later, at the age of 18, Champ fathered his second child. Champ told Schwab that he is still in contact with both children and their mothers.

Two-Way College Star

In 1995 Champ was the top high-school football recruit in Georgia. With Ronald already at the University of Georgia, there was no question where Champ was headed for college, however. On graduating

During his three seasons with the University of Georgia Bulldogs, Champ was a key member of the team. He played as a wide receiver on offense, intercepted passes as a defensive back, and even returned punts and kickoffs.

from Charlton County High School, Champ followed his older brother to the University of Georgia.

In his freshman year, 1996, Champ appeared in every game for the Georgia Bulldogs, although he did not play much. Beginning in his sophomore year, however, Champ played wide receiver, cornerback, and kick returner. In an article by Michael Bradley in *The Sporting News*, Greg Williams, a University of Georgia football coach, spoke about Champ:

> **"From the minute he stepped onto the field, it was obvious he was the best athlete out there. . . . He would do things during practice that made you shake your head."**

In a game against Louisiana State University, Champ showed his ability to dominate. In the first quarter, Champ caught a pass for a touchdown, one of his seven total catches for 114 yards. He ran the ball twice for 15 yards and also returned three kickoffs for 66 yards. On defense, Champ took part in 47 of the Bulldogs' 61 plays, helping limit the Tigers to six points in the second half. In total, Champ was involved in 96 plays in the game. Eventually, Champ became known as the best two-way player—that is, one who plays both offense and defense—in the country.

Champ capped his junior year with the Bulldogs' 35–33 Peach Bowl victory over the University of Virginia Cavaliers in December 1998. In addition to catching three passes for 73 yards and a touchdown, Champ had a great defensive game, for which he was named the game's most valuable defensive player.

CROSS-CURRENTS

Read "Georgia's Football Program" to learn more about the long and proud history of the sport at the university. Go to page 48. ▶▶

At the end of the 1998 season, Champ won the Bronko Nagurski Trophy, which is awarded each year to the nation's top defensive college player. He was also named a first team All-American.

After his junior season, Champ decided he was ready for professional football. He declared himself eligible for the 1999 NFL **draft**.

CHAMP TURNS PRO

On the day of the 1999 National Football League draft, NFL commissioner Paul Tagliabue announced that the Washington Redskins had chosen Champ Bailey, cornerback from the University of Georgia, for their team. The Redskins took Champ with the seventh pick of the draft. With that announcement, Champ Bailey's professional football career officially began.

The Redskins obviously felt that Champ was going to be a special player. After drafting Champ, the Redskins released Chris Dishman, a cornerback who had gone to the Pro Bowl two seasons earlier, but whose skills had begun to decline. Washington's head coach, Norv Turner, said that Champ would only play on defense until he was comfortable with the speed of NFL games.

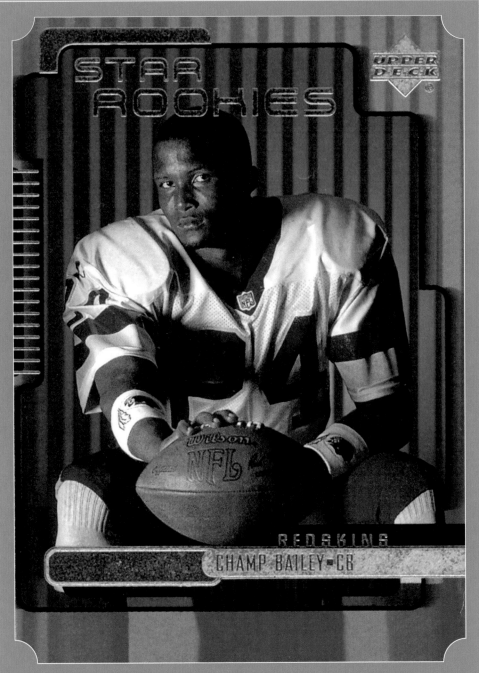

STAR ROOKIES

REDSKINS
CHAMP BAILEY·CB

A trading card from Champ's rookie year. The Washington Redskins selected Champ with the seventh pick in the 1999 NFL draft. Champ worked hard in training camp and earned a spot in the Redskins' starting lineup.

Redskins head coach Norv Turner (pictured) decided not to let Champ play with Washington's offense. Turner felt that Champ needed to focus on playing defense so he could adjust to the speed of the NFL.

A Veteran Teacher

For Champ, one of the best things about being drafted by the Redskins was that he would get to work with the team's veteran cornerback, Darrell Green. Dennis Tuttle of *The Sporting News* pointed out that in 1983, Green's rookie season in the NFL, Champ had been in kindergarten. Tuttle described the association between Green and Champ as a "student-teacher relationship" in which Bailey eagerly sought advice from the future Hall of Famer. Tuttle quoted Champ on his feelings about working with Darrell Green:

> **"I was anxious to meet him and get to know him. . . . . When we did meet [at mini-camp in April], he said that I could ask him anything about being on or off the field. When he said that, I took his word for it and started asking him things."**

Many top draft picks come into the National Football League thinking they know all there is to know about football. However, playing in the NFL is not the same as playing in college. In the pros, every player is as good or better than the top college players. Rookies who come into the league unwilling to learn and work hard do not last long. Champ understood this from the beginning. He told Tuttle:

CROSS-CURRENTS

Check out "Average Career Length" to find out how long the average NFL player can expect to be in the league. Go to page 50. ▶▶

"Coming out of college, I figured there would be a lot of things I didn't know. But I didn't know how much. I'm a little surprised it's as deep as it is. Some of the things Darrell was looking at [on film] were things I'd never thought of. Like, if this guy lines up here, it's almost certain he's going to run this route. And he probably won't get the ball."

Redskin Rookie

Champ did so well in practice and preseason play that he was in Washington's starting lineup by the time the 1999 season began. Although he left the season opener with a leg cramp, Champ soon began showing his skills on the field. In the third game of the season, two big plays by Champ helped the Redskins beat the New York Jets, 27–20. First, Champ tackled the Jets' Kevin Williams. Williams had carried a kickoff back for 81 yards, but Champ stopped him from scoring. On the next play, Jets quarterback Rick Mirer passed to receiver Keyshawn Johnson in the end zone. Champ was able to break up the pass and keep the Jets from scoring.

It was only the first month of the season, and Champ was already having a big impact. Before Champ had joined the Redskins, opposing teams would stay away from Darrell Green's side of the field. According to Tuttle, once the other teams saw Champ play, they began taking their chances with Green:

"Just one month into the season, Bailey's progress has been so steady that he not only is starting at one of the game's most demanding positions but also is making

opponents do something the Redskins haven't seen in years: challenge Green's side of the field. "

Champ learned fast. In the Redskins' first four games, he was matched up against four tough receivers—the Dallas Cowboys' Michael Irvin, the New York Giants' Amani Toomer, the Jets' Keyshawn Johnson, and the Carolina Panthers' Muhsin Muhammad. After giving up a few early catches to each, Champ figured out how to shut them down.

Champ grabs an interception during Washington's training camp in the summer of 1999. As a rookie, Champ had an opportunity to learn from teammate Darrell Green, one of the best cornerbacks in the game.

The Redskins' first game against the Arizona Cardinals was a highlight of Champ's rookie season. In the second quarter, Champ intercepted a pass from Cardinals' quarterback Jake Plummer. He ran the pick back for a touchdown—his first in the NFL. Later in the game, he intercepted two more passes by Cardinals quarterbacks. At just 21 years of age, Champ became the youngest player in the NFL ever to make three interceptions in one game.

The Redskins finished the 1999 season with a 10–6 record. That was good enough to win the National Football Conference (NFC) East division title. Washington headed to the first round of the playoffs to face the Detroit Lions. The Redskins led the whole game. In the second quarter, when it looked as if the Lions were about to score, Champ intercepted a pass by Detroit quarterback Gus Frerotte. The Lions never threatened after that, and the Redskins won easily, 27–13.

The Redskins lost their next playoff game to the Tampa Bay Buccaneers, 14–13. However, it had been a great rookie season for Champ Bailey. During the 1999 season, Champ made 73 solo tackles and assisted on six others. He had a **sack** and five interceptions. Champ was off to a great start in the NFL. According to the *Sporting News*, Darrell Green said of Champ:

> **❝What I'm proud of the most about him is the way he has competed. These are the things I look for: how you bounce back, how you deal with success, how you deal with failure and how you do the whole job. And that affects the whole team.❞**

A Tough Second Season

In Champ's second season with Washington, the team added a great player who would help with the young cornerback's development. Legendary cornerback Deion Sanders signed with the Redskins after being released by the Dallas Cowboys. Although Sanders was not as good as he once had been, having him on the team was great for Champ. In addition to learning from Darrell Green, Champ could also learn from the player nicknamed "Prime Time" because of his ability to make big plays.

The 2000 season turned out to be filled with ups and downs for the Redskins. The Redskins won six of their first eight games, and seemed likely to win the division title again. However, Washington only won two more games the rest of the season, finishing at 8–8. As a result, head coach Norv Turner was fired after 13 games. Terry Robiskie replaced him.

Despite his team's problems, Champ played well. In the season's first game, Champ had eight tackles. He also made an important defensive play that prevented Panthers kick returner Michael Bates from scoring a touchdown. In Washington's second game, a 15–10 loss to Detroit, Champ had two interceptions, but it was not enough to change the outcome. Against the Cowboys, Champ made a long punt return, but the Redskins fell behind Dallas and could not catch up. In a game against the Philadelphia Eagles, Champ intercepted a pass, but Washington lost, 23–20.

CROSS-CURRENTS

To learn more about the challenges facing athletes who play on both offense and defense, read "Playing Both Ways." Go to page 51. ▶▶

The Redskins ended the disappointing 2000 season on a good note with a 20–3 victory over the Arizona Cardinals. This was a huge game for Champ, who excelled on both offense and defense. On offense, Champ scored a touchdown on a seven-yard run, and he also caught two passes and returned punts. On defense, Champ intercepted a pass in the end zone. For the year, Champ recorded five interceptions, 57 solo tackles, five assists, and a **fumble** recovery. His excellent performance earned him his first trip to the Pro Bowl.

Keeping It Up

The 2001 season was also tough for Champ and the Redskins. The team's record again was only 8–8. Champ, however, had another strong season, with three interceptions, a fumble recovery, 49 solo tackles, two assists, and a second Pro Bowl selection.

For Champ Bailey, the most significant event of the next year occurred before the football season began. In May 2002, Champ married Hanady Aboneeaj, his longtime girlfriend. Champ and Hanady had met while they were both attending the University of Georgia. A number of former and current NFL players, including Larry Centers, Steven Davis, Deion Sanders, and Troy Vincent, attended the wedding. Wide receiver Irving Fryar, an ordained Pentecostal minister, performed the ceremony.

Champ tackles Philadelphia wide receiver Torrance Small during a November 2000 home game. Although Champ intercepted a pass during the game, the Eagles won, 23–20. This was one of eight losses for the Redskins in 2000.

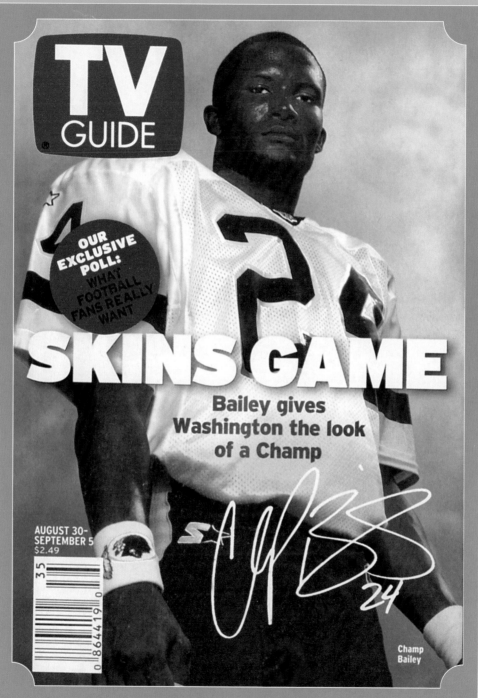

TV GUIDE

OUR EXCLUSIVE POLL: WHAT FOOTBALL FANS REALLY WANT

SKINS GAME

Bailey gives Washington the look of a Champ

AUGUST 30–
SEPTEMBER 5
$2.49

Champ Bailey

0 86441 9

By the end of the 2002 season, Champ was recognized as one of the best cornerbacks in the NFL. He was selected for the NFC's Pro Bowl team in 2000, 2001, 2002, and 2003.

Like 2001, the 2002 season was disappointing for the Redskins. The team finished with a 7–9 record. Champ, however, kept getting better. As a punt returner, Champ gained 238 yards on 24 chances, an average of nearly 10 yards per return. Playing cornerback, he had three interceptions, a fumble recovery, 62 solo tackles, six assists, and a career-high 24 passes defended. (This means that Champ knocked the ball away from the receiver 24 times.) Again, Champ went to the Pro Bowl.

One of the few highlights during the difficult 2002 season came in Washington's final game. The Redskins' 20–14 victory over Dallas ended a streak of 10 straight losses to the Cowboys. The win sent Champ's mentor, Darrell Green, into retirement on a positive note. In the final game of Green's career, the Redskins used a trick play in which Champ caught a punt, then handed off the ball to Green, who ran for 35 yards. After the game, Champ said:

"Now I know how it feels to beat the Cowboys. Beating them and sending Darrell off with a win—you can't do much better than that."

Another Disappointing Season

Although Champ struggled with various injuries during the 2003 season, his performance was still strong. With two interceptions, two fumble recoveries, 68 solo tackles, and four assists, he was again selected for the Pro Bowl.

In the fourth week of the 2003 season, Champ showed his toughness. Playing the New England Patriots, Champ intercepted a pass and forced a fumble. He made these big plays despite a sprained left shoulder and a broken left wrist. Champ's plays contributed to the Redskins' 20–17 win.

In the 15th week of the season, however, Champ's season came to an early end when he suffered a concussion and a bad cut on his face while trying to prevent a touchdown by the Chicago Bears. It would be Champ's last play as a Redskin.

A NEW UNIFORM FOR CHAMP

Although Champ played well in 2003, the Redskins finished with a terrible 5–11 record. After Champ's first season with the team, the Redskins had been unable to put together a winning season. From 2000 to 2003, the Redskins won 28 games and lost 36. One problem may have been that the team changed its head coach almost every year.

Champ's numbers for his first five years in the NFL were impressive. Champ had intercepted 18 passes and had been credited with 82 passes defended in his career. In four out of five seasons, he had been chosen to play in the Pro Bowl. Quarterbacks rarely threw to Champ's side of the field. When they did,

Champ dives for a pass during a Redskins game. Although the star cornerback had played well during his first five seasons in the NFL, Washington was unable to reach the playoffs after Champ's rookie year.

Champ often made them pay. Champ was a major contributor to his team and one of the top defensive players in the NFL.

After being drafted, Champ had signed a five-year contract with the Redskins. His contract ended after the 2003 season. Before the 2003 season began, Champ's **agent** went to the Redskins looking for a new deal. Washington offered Champ a nine-year, $55 million contract. However, Champ turned down this offer. He felt that he deserved to make more money.

The Big Trade

In February 2004, the Redskins gave Champ permission to see whether another team wanted him. Rumors began almost immediately that the Denver Broncos were interested. By early March, the

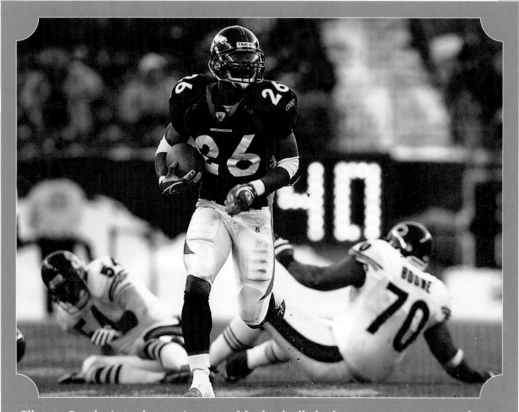

Clinton Portis (number 26) runs with the ball during a 2003 game against Chicago. Portis was an up-and-coming NFL star. In each of his two seasons with the Broncos, Portis rushed for more than 1,500 yards.

two teams had made a trade deal. The Redskins would send Champ to the Broncos. The Broncos would send Clinton Portis, their young star running back, to Washington. The Broncos would also get the Redskins' second-round pick in the next NFL draft.

The trade was huge news in the football world for a couple of reasons. The first was that both Champ and Clinton Portis were Pro Bowl–quality players. The second was the money. The Redskins gave Portis a nine-year, $50.5 million contract. The Broncos and Champ agreed upon a seven-year, $63 million contract. Champ received an $18 million bonus for signing the deal, and $5 million in other bonuses. It was the biggest contract the Broncos had given any player. It was also the biggest contract ever given to an NFL cornerback.

Many in the media felt that the Broncos had gotten the best of the trade. The Broncos' main goal had been to get rid of Portis, a player who was unhappy with his contract. To be able to trade Portis for a top cornerback and a high draft pick was very fortunate, especially since Denver was able to pick up running back Tatum Bell with Washington's second-round draft pick. According to Lee Rasizer of the *Rocky Mountain News*,

CROSS-CURRENTS

If you want to learn more about how pro football players are paid, read "NFL Player Salaries." Go to page 51. ▶▶

> **"A happy medium ultimately left two organizations largely pleased. Running back Clinton Portis' contract demands in Denver, Champ Bailey's discontent . . . in Washington and the needs of the two clubs were neatly addressed in one of the biggest deals in NFL history."**

For his part, Champ approached his new team with enthusiasm and confidence. Writing for *DenverBroncos.com*, Andrew Mason quoted Champ as saying,

> **"I can promise one thing to the owner, the coach, and my teammates—that they'll get 110 percent out of me every day. . . . I will be a class guy, I will do the right thing, and I won't be a disappointment, I can guarantee that."**

Champ's agent, Jack Reale, confirmed Champ's enthusiasm in an Associated Press article:

> **❝I think Champ's really ecstatic. . . . He's happy to be playing for [Denver coach] Mike Shanahan and happy about the stability of the Broncos organization.❞**

A New Start

It did not take long for Champ to make an impact on his new team. In their first game of the 2004 season, the Broncos played the Kansas City Chiefs. Champ contributed to the Broncos' 34–24 victory with a pass defended and an interception. He also caught a pass for an 11-yard gain while playing offense.

The new season also had its rough spots, however. Playing the Cincinnati Bengals in week seven, Champ had a tough time covering Chad Johnson, the Bengals' flashy wide receiver. Although Champ intercepted one pass, Johnson made several catches, including a 50-yard touchdown, against Champ in man-to-man coverage.

Overall, though, Champ's first season with the Broncos was a success. Champ had three interceptions, 68 solo tackles, and 13 assists. He was again invited to play in the Pro Bowl.

CROSS-CURRENTS

To learn about a rule that affects the way cornerbacks defend against wide receivers, read "The Illegal Contact Rule." Go to page 52. ▶▶

Denver finished with a 10–6 record in 2004. This was Champ's first winning season in many years. When asked about the big trade that brought him to the Broncos, Champ expressed the importance of winning. He told Jon Robinson of ign.com:

> **❝I think both teams got what they wanted, what they needed. You hate to lose a Clinton Portis, you hate to lose a Champ Bailey, but at the same time, we're winning and [Washington is] not. It really doesn't matter who got the better end, I'm on the better team and that's all that matters.❞**

The Broncos advanced to the playoffs, where they faced the Indianapolis Colts. Although the Broncos had beaten the Colts in a recent game, the Colts were one of the best teams in the NFL. In the playoff game, Colts quarterback Peyton Manning passed for 457 yards, and the Colts scored a team playoff record seven touchdowns. The Colts knocked the Broncos out of the playoffs, 49–24.

Champ breaks up a pass intended for Jacksonville's Jimmy Smith during a 2004 game. Champ had another good season in 2004. His work on Denver's defense helped the Broncos win 10 games and reach the playoffs.

The Colts' Dallas Clark makes a catch in front of Champ during the January 9, 2005, playoff game between Indianapolis and Denver. Champ had seven tackles during the game. However, the Colts overwhelmed the Broncos, 49–24.

The Best Cornerback In the NFL

Writing about the effect Champ had on the Broncos in his first season with the team, Jon Robinson noted:

❝Champ Bailey has not only changed the way the Broncos play [defense], he's transformed the entire attitude of the defense into a crew who can make decisive plays with the game on the line.

> **The Broncos defense finally has some swagger to it, and they owe it all to Champ.**"

Having Champ on defense made calling plays much harder for opposing quarterbacks. He guarded wide receivers so well that the quarterbacks thought twice about passing to them. According to Broncos defensive coordinator Larry Coyer, the Broncos chose to have Champ play man-to-man coverage on the opponents' best wide receiver in 11 out of their 17 games during 2004. In those games, Champ held the wide receiver against whom he was matched below that receiver's average number of catches and yards nearly 75 percent of the time.

Back to School

Champ did not limit himself to football. In 2004 he returned to the University of Georgia in the off-season. Even though he had earned plenty of money as a football player, he still wanted to complete a college degree in psychology. He spoke to *Sports Illustrated* about taking classes and the importance of education:

> **"It's definitely more challenging to be in school now. You don't have anybody pushing you. You don't have to do it in order to be eligible. The desire has to come from within. It's made me respect the regular students because they have to lean on that education to get through life. It's not like I'm in a position where I have to go back and do that.**"

Going Further

The 2005 season did not start well for Champ and the Broncos. Playing the Miami Dolphins in their season opener, the Broncos lost, 34–10. To make things worse, Champ had to leave the game in the third quarter with a separated shoulder. The Broncos' next game, against the San Diego Chargers, also did not start well. At halftime, the Broncos were down 14–3. At the beginning of the third quarter, however, Champ intercepted a pass by Chargers quarterback Drew Brees and ran the ball back for a touchdown. Denver ended the game with a 20–13 victory.

In the following weeks, Champ struggled with a hamstring injury. His hamstring was bothering him so much that he did not play at all against the Jacksonville Jaguars. This was the start of a rare period in Champ's career of his not starting games or sitting out significant portions of games because of injuries. Although he was back two weeks later, he could not play the whole game because his hamstring was still bothering him.

Champ runs an interception back 25 yards for a touchdown against the Chargers, September 18, 2005. The pick gave Denver its first win of the season. The Broncos would finish 2005 with a 13-3 record and another playoff berth.

By the seventh week of the season, Champ was again playing good football. In the Broncos' 24–23 loss to the New York Giants, Champ intercepted a pass by Giants quarterback Eli Manning.

Back in Top Form

For the rest of the season, the Broncos were a powerhouse team. They lost only one more regular-season game. During this great run, Champ was one of the Broncos' key players. Playing against the Oakland Raiders, Champ intercepted a pass by Kerry Collins, helping the Broncos to a 31–17 win. The next week, against the New York Jets, he made his fifth interception of the season. Over the next three weeks, Champ made three more interceptions. With a streak of five interceptions in as many games, Champ set a team record.

The Broncos ended 2005 with a 13–3 record, winning their division. In the first round of the playoffs, they beat the New England Patriots, 27–13. It was a dramatic game for Champ. With the Patriots on the Broncos' five-yard line, Champ intercepted a pass by New England quarterback Tom Brady and ran 101 yards to the Patriots' goal line before losing control of the ball. His teammate Mike Anderson scored the touchdown on the next play, giving the Broncos a 17–6 lead. Champ's 101-yard run went down in NFL history as the longest interception return not to end in a touchdown.

The Bronco's next playoff game was the American Football Conference (AFC) championship game. The Broncos' luck ran out when they lost a tough game to the Pittsburgh Steelers. Although the Steelers stopped the Broncos short of making the Super Bowl, there was no denying that Champ's team had a very strong season. The Broncos' defensive backfield made a total of 19 interceptions for the season—eight of them by Champ. Champ scored two touchdowns, and also had 23 passes defended, 60 solo tackles, and six assists. On the strength of these numbers, Champ made the Pro Bowl for the sixth time in his career.

STILL THE CHAMP

After making the playoffs in the previous two years—and making it to the AFC finals following the 2005 season—Champ and the Broncos were hoping for an even better season in 2006. Denver added some players in the offseason that many people thought would significantly improve the team. Champ seemed happy to be a Bronco.

Toward the end of the Broncos' strong 2005 season, Champ expressed appreciation for the Broncos fans. He told Jon Robinson of ign.com:

"I think you kind of feed off the crowd. They definitely give me a lot of energy. When they are right

behind you, pumping you up with everything they have got, it makes you want to play a little harder. When you feed off that, it definitely helps you win games. **"**

Picking Off Opponents

For the first nine games of 2006, it looked as though the Broncos were on track for another great season. In mid-November, Denver's record was 7–2. Champ made game-changing plays nearly every week. In a 13–3 win over the Baltimore Ravens, he leaped high in the end zone to intercept a pass by Ravens quarterback Steve McNair. The following week, Champ intercepted another pass to stop a scoring drive by the Oakland Raiders.

The Broncos enter their stadium before a 2006 game. After their great 2005 season, Denver had high expectations for 2006. Champ had five interceptions in the team's first nine games, helping the Broncos win seven of those contests.

Playing the Cleveland Browns in the seventh week of the season, Champ picked off a pass by Browns quarterback Charlie Frye in the end zone, preventing the Browns from scoring. When the Browns finally did score a touchdown in the fourth quarter, it came as a surprise. Champ and the rest of the Broncos defense had been so effective at shutting opponents down that it was only the second touchdown scored against them all season.

One of the Broncos' only losses in the first half of the 2006 season came against the Indianapolis Colts, the team that had knocked them out of the playoffs the previous year. Although the Broncos lost, 34–31, Champ had a super game. He defended Colts star receiver Marvin Harrison so well that Harrison managed just five catches for 38 yards—well below his season averages. Unfortunately,

Champ blocks a pass intended for Pittsburgh's Hines Ward, November 5, 2006. During the game against the Steelers, Champ intercepted two passes and knocked down five others as the Broncos won, 31–20.

Colts quarterback Peyton Manning also had another receiver, Reggie Wayne, to whom he could pass. Manning was able to complete 10 passes to Wayne for 138 yards and three touchdowns.

After the game, Manning—one of the best quarterbacks in the NFL—commented on Champ's ability to shut down receivers and intercept passes. Manning said that when he practiced with his receivers during the offseason, he had tough cornerbacks like Champ in mind:

> **"That's why you throw a lot in the off-season, with nobody covering. You pretend it's Champ Bailey covering. You have to throw a perfect throw and run a perfect route."**

Good Turns Bad

Another top quarterback, the Pittsburgh Steelers' Ben Roethlisberger, learned the hard way how tough it is to get a throw past Champ. When the Broncos played the Steelers in the ninth week of the season, Champ intercepted two of Roethlisberger's passes at the three-yard line. Champ stopped the Steelers from closing the score. The Broncos kept the lead for a 31–20 win.

Although the Broncos won again the next week against Oakland, that victory marked the high point of the season. The rest of the season was a disaster. Denver had five losses—including a four-game losing streak—and only two more wins. Through this discouraging period, Champ still had some good games. In the Broncos' 23–20 loss to the Seattle Seahawks, he picked off his sixth pass of the season. In each of the Broncos' wins against the Arizona Cardinals and the Cincinnati Bengals, he contributed more interceptions.

Champ provided another highlight in the last game of the 2006 season. Playing against the San Francisco 49ers, Champ grabbed his 10th interception of the season and ran the ball 70 yards for a huge touchdown. Champ's touchdown gave the Broncos a 13–0 lead in a game the team had to win in order to make the playoffs. However, the 49ers came back and won the game, 26–23. The Broncos ended the season with a 9–7 record.

In spite of the Broncos' troubles in the second half of the season, Champ Bailey had put on a brilliant performance during 2006. His

10 interceptions tied him with the New England Patriots' Asante Samuel for the most in the league. He also had a fumble recovery and 74 solo tackles. For his achievements, he was chosen to go to the Pro Bowl for the seventh year in a row.

Tough Season in 2007

If the 2006 season was hard for the Broncos, the 2007 season was even harder. Long before the football season began, Champ's team suffered great tragedy and loss. Within the first two months of 2007, two of Champ's teammates died. First, their starting right cornerback, Darrent Williams, was shot and killed on New Year's Day when his stretch limousine was sprayed with bullets in a drive-by shooting. Then, backup running back Damien Nash collapsed and died following a charity basketball game.

Another issue for the team centered on the quarterback position. In 2006, the team had switched quarterbacks from Jake Plummer to Jay Cutler. The veteran Plummer had been struggling, and the Broncos management saw Cutler as the team's future. At first, Cutler was an improvement over Plummer. Toward the end of the 2006 season, however, Cutler also had trouble on the field. It was later discovered that Cutler suffers from Type 1 diabetes. The disease had caused him to lose 35 pounds and a great deal of strength. With proper medication and diet Cutler was able to continue to play football.

Champ's Continued Brilliance

Amid all the turmoil on the team, the Broncos' coach, Mike Shanahan, expressed confidence in Champ:

> **"Champ's a guy that works every day, and he's not content just being a great player. He wants to be the best player. And when he practices, it shows."**

Champ Bailey continued his brilliant cornerback play in the 2007 season. Although he missed one game completely and played with an injured **quadriceps** in two other games, Champ consistently made big plays that either helped the Broncos seal a win or hold off an opponent threatening to take the lead. After leading the league in

Champ covers a Buffalo Bills wide receiver during the first game of the 2007 season. The Broncos won the opener, but struggled in the following weeks. Denver finished with a 7–9 record and missed the playoffs.

interceptions with 10 in 2006, Champ's interception total fell to only three in 2007. However, the number dropped in part because quarterbacks often refused to throw to Champ's side of the field. Champ made 71 solo tackles—the second most on the team—and was chosen for the Pro Bowl for the eighth time in a row.

Broncos defensive coordinator Jim Bates pointed out the importance of Champ's tackling ability:

❝He's the most complete cornerback I've been around. His tackling is the difference.❞

In a Broncos press release about his eighth Pro Bowl selection, however, Champ showed that team accomplishments are as important to him as personal achievements:

"It's a little bittersweet because we haven't met our team expectations for the season, but it's an honor to be respected around the league and by fans."

Champ's Team Spirit

Despite Champ's strong play, the Broncos finished with a losing record, seven wins and nine losses, in 2007. After the season, the team's management made many changes. A number of players were traded, released, or allowed to leave the team as free agents. One of them was kicker Jason Elam, who had spent 15 seasons with Denver.

As the Broncos worked to move past their troubles in 2007, Champ took on the role of team leader. He spoke about his commitment to building a winning team in Denver. He talked to younger players, and tried to teach them what they would need to do to succeed in the NFL.

One change in the Broncos' roster was particularly exciting for Champ. In March 2008, Denver signed his younger brother, Boss, to play linebacker for the team. Boss Bailey had been playing for the Detroit Lions since 2003. Champ was thrilled for the chance to play in the same defense as his brother. He said:

CROSS-CURRENTS

To learn about a rule change that may affect Champ's play in the 2008 season, read "No More Sideline 'Force-Outs.'" Go to page 53. ▶▶

"[Boss] brings athleticism, he'll make some plays, and that's big for us. . . . They didn't use him right in Detroit. We're going to use him right here. I'll make sure of that."

CROSS-CURRENTS

Read "Brothers in the NFL" to learn more about some siblings who have succeeded in the NFL. Go to page 54. ▶▶

Continued Excellence

Champ Bailey has yet to achieve one of his biggest goals—victory in the Super Bowl. However, throughout his career he has consistently held a place among the league's top players.

In an article in *Sports Illustrated for Kids*, some of Champ's teammates and coaches told Gary Gramling how much they respect Champ. According to Gramling, Broncos safety Nick Ferguson said of Champ,

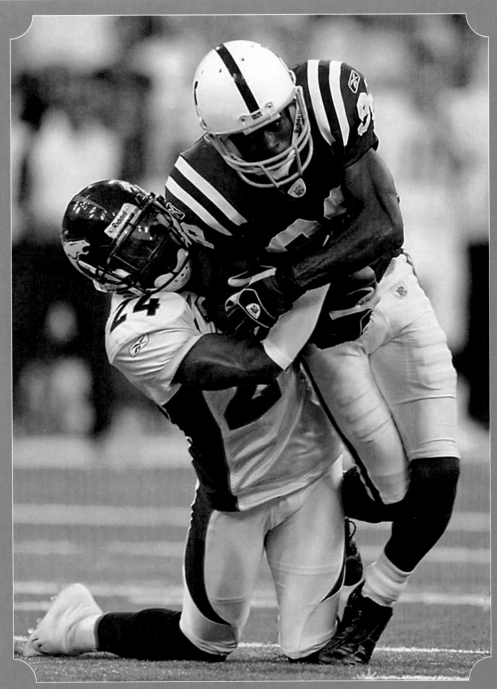

Lions' receiver Shaun McDonald can't get away from Champ, and is stopped after a short gain. Champ remains the NFL's premiere cover cornerback. Often, quarterbacks will not throw to his side of the field.

Champ waves to fans during a practice for the 2008 Pro Bowl, played in Honolulu, Hawaii. Champ was selected to the NFL's all-star game eight times in his first nine seasons.

"He sees everything. . . . I've seen him intercept passes nowhere near the play when it started. Champ leads the league in instincts.**"**

Champ prides himself on having the right instincts to make big plays. In 2006, he told *USA Today*,

"I don't go out of my way [to make big plays]. . . . It's got to go with my role on the defense, but sometimes I'll see something that's about to happen, and I trust my instincts. I mean, that's really why I'm here. I have the athletic ability, and I have those instincts to make those plays.**"**

In an article in Denver's *Rocky Mountain News*, written at the end of the 2007 season, sportswriter Jeff Legwold called Champ the Broncos' most valuable defensive player. Legwold also said that Champ remains among the top players in the NFL:

"Champ Bailey simply, consistently, affects more of what opposing offenses do than any other Broncos defender.

He tackles better than any cornerback in the league, better than almost any who have been in the league at the position. He studies, he plays beginning to end and he affects play despite the fact most offenses don't even bother to look his way.**"**

Champ Bailey has already accomplished many things on the football field. Given his immense physical ability, his tremendous work ethic, and his dedication to improving his team, it is a safe bet that Champ will remain a superstar of pro football for years to come.

America's Most Popular Sport

In the United States, baseball is known as the "national pastime," and it has always been popular. In 1985, however, Harris Interactive, a marketing-research company, took a poll to find out what sport was the most popular in the country. The winner was professional football. Each year since then, pro football has polled the highest in popularity in the United States. According to the most recent Harris Interactive poll, 30 percent of sports fans polled in 2008 rank it as their favorite sport, up from 24 percent in 1985. Baseball ranked second in popularity in the Harris poll.

Going to football games is a popular activity. Anyone, however, can watch football on television. Some TV stations show football games on Saturday and Sunday mornings, afternoons, and evenings. Football fans can also watch Monday night football and sometimes even Thursday night football. Some football fans buy special football television packages that allow them to watch college and pro football games from around the country. The biggest football event of the year is the Super Bowl—the championship game of the NFL. The Super Bowl is usually not only the most watched NFL game of the year, it is also nearly always the most watched TV broadcast of the year. (Go back to page 6.) ◀◀

The Washington Redskins play a game before a sold-out crowd at their home field. The Redskins' football stadium is the largest in the NFL. It can seat more than 91,000 fans.

Great Cornerbacks

Many people think cornerback is the hardest position to play in football. Good cornerbacks have to be able to defend against all types of receivers. Some receivers are tall and have long arms that seem to simply pluck the football out of the sky. Others are extremely fast. Some run perfect, precise routes and make their **cuts** quickly. Before many defenders can react, the quarterback passes the football right into their hands. Some receivers are so strong that, once they have the ball, they are hard to tackle. Other receivers are able to get away from defenders. The best cornerbacks need to be fast, strong, and smart enough to keep the ball away from the top receivers.

In addition to Champ Bailey, the list of great NFL cornerbacks includes Deion Sanders and Darrell Green. Both Sanders and Green helped inspire Champ.

Darrell Green

Darrell Green entered the NFL in 1983 and played until 2002. He shares the record for most seasons played with one team, playing all 20 of his NFL seasons with the Washington Redskins. During his career, Green made 54 interceptions, returning them for 621 yards and six touchdowns. Green was well known for his speed. He is said to have run the fastest 40-yard dash of any NFL player.

One of the highlights of Green's career was the Redskins' 1987 playoff game against the Chicago Bears. In this game, Green returned a punt 52 yards to score the game-winning touchdown. During his career, Green made the Pro Bowl seven times and was picked as an All-Pro player four times. Green was elected into the Pro Football Hall of Fame in 2008.

Deion Sanders

Unlike Green, Deion Sanders played for many teams during his 14-year NFL career, including the Atlanta Falcons, San Francisco 49ers, Dallas Cowboys, Washington Redskins, and Baltimore Ravens. Sanders was such a feared defensive player that some coaches told their quarterbacks not to pass to his side of the field. During his career, Sanders made 53 interceptions and 513 tackles. He made the Pro Bowl eight times and was picked for the All-Pro team nine times. In addition to his success in the NFL, Sanders also played major league baseball. He had a .263 career batting average, appearing in more than 600 games with the New York Yankees, Atlanta Braves, Cincinnati Reds, and San Francisco Giants.

"Shutdown" Cornerbacks

Great cornerbacks such as Deion Sanders, Darrell Green, and Champ Bailey are often called "shutdown" cornerbacks because they make it nearly impossible for opponents to make a play on their sides of the field.

(Go back to page 7.)

Nicknames

Like players in other professional sports leagues, some NFL players are known by nicknames. Some of these players got their nicknames when they were young, usually from their families. Other players acquired their nicknames while in school. Still others did not get their nicknames until they made it to the pros.

Some players' nicknames have to do with how they look. Some relate to a player's personality or lifestyle, others to the person's style of play, and others are derived from a player's name. Some players like their nicknames. Others may not like their nickname at all, and may even ask people not to call them by that name.

Here is a list of the nicknames of some past and present NFL players:

Bambi (Lance Alworth)	Boomer (Norman Esiason)	Sweetness (Walter Payton)
Snake (Ken Stabler)	The Bus (Jerome Bettis)	The Ghost (Dave Casper)
Boss (Rodney Bailey)	Cadillac (Carnell Williams)	The Golden Boy (Paul Hornung)
Broadway Joe (Joe Namath)	Deuce (Dulymus McAllister)	The Horse (Alan Ameche)
Champ (Roland Bailey, Jr.)	Hacksaw (Jack Reynolds)	Refrigerator (William Perry)
Crazy Legs (Elroy Hirsch)	Ickey (Elbert Woods)	The Minister of Defense
Flipper (Willie Anderson)	Jumbo (James Eliot)	(Reggie White)
Frenchy (John Fuqua)	Jumpy (James Geathers)	Joe Cool (Joe Montana)
Diesel (John Riggins)	Night Train (Dick Lane)	Too Tall (Ed Jones)
The Mad Stork (Ted	Neon or Prime Time (Deion	
Hendricks)	Sanders)	

(Go back to page 12.)

Georgia's Football Program

The University of Georgia (UGA) Bulldogs football program has a long and proud history. Over the years, the Bulldogs have fielded some of the best college football teams in the country.

A History of Great Coaches

Glenn "Pop" Warner coached the team from 1895 to 1896 and led UGA to its first undefeated season (4–0). From 1923 to 1927, George Cecil "Kid" Woodruff coached the UGA football team. Woodruff, who had been captain of the 1911 team, brought a new style of offense to the school and led UGA to the Southern Conference championship in 1927. In 1938, Wally Butts was hired as an assistant by football coach Joel Hunt. Hunt quit the following year, and Butts became the head coach. Butts built the Bulldogs into a national football power over the next 22 years. One highlight of Butts' career came when the Bulldogs won the 1959 Southeastern Conference championship.

Vince Dooley led the Bulldogs to more than 200 victories between 1964 and 1988—more than any other Bulldogs coach. He was named NCAA National Coach of the Year in 1980 and 1982, was honored as Southeastern Conference Coach of the Year seven times, and was presented the Amos Alonzo Stagg award in 2001. Dooley's commitment to academics was as strong as his commitment to winning football games. While he was coach, seven Bulldogs players earned prestigious National Football Foundation postgraduate scholarships and 11 former players received NCAA postgraduate scholarships. Seventy-seven of Dooley's players earned Academic All-SEC recognition.

A Pipeline to the Pros

According to the UGA media guide, the NFL has drafted more than 230 Bulldogs. More than 40 former UGA players have appeared in the Super Bowl, and 25 different former Bulldogs players have won the NFL's championship—several more than once. As of 2008, 41 former Georgia players were active in the NFL. This trailed only Florida State University (45) and the University of Miami (44).

Among the most notable former Bulldogs are Heisman Trophy winner Herschel Walker, Outland Trophy winner Bill Stanfill, All-Americans Fran Tarkenton and Pat Dye, Super Bowl MVPs Jake Scott, Terrell Davis, and Hines Ward, and outstanding cornerback Champ Bailey. A total of 27 former Bulldogs have been voted to the Pro Bowl, including Champ Bailey (eight times), Richard Seymour (five times), Mack Strong (two times), and Marcus Stroud (three times). Twenty-three former Bulldogs have played 10 seasons or more in the NFL. Former Bulldog Ray Donaldson's NFL career lasted 17 years—more than four times the average length of an NFL career.

(Go back to page 15.)

The Bulldogs play at their home field, Sanford Stadium, in Athens, Georgia. The school's football program is one of the oldest in the country. Since 1892, the university's football teams have won more than 700 games.

Average Career Length

Some NFL players have long careers in the league. Washington Redskins cornerback Darrell Green played for 20 seasons. In 2008, quarterback Brett Favre returned for his 18th NFL season. All of these great players, however, come up short against George Blanda, who played for an incredible 26 seasons.

George Blanda was a quarterback and placekicker who played for five teams during his 26-year NFL career. At the time he retired, Blanda had scored more points than any other player in league history.

In contrast to the few players who stay in the NFL for a decade or more, there are many players who play one or two seasons and either get cut or suffer a career-ending injury. According to a study by the NFL Player's Association, an average NFL career lasts only 3.33 years. Many players of certain positions average even shorter careers. Cornerbacks averaged 2.94 years, followed by wide receivers at 2.81 years. Running backs have the shortest average career length, at only 2.57 years. The NFL Player's Association says that the reason these players have such short careers is the "high-speed collisions" they endure while playing.

On the other hand, quarterbacks, punters, and kickers have the longest average career lengths. Punters and kickers are only on the field for a few plays each game. Blockers and league rules protect quarterbacks. The average career length for an NFL quarterback is 4.44 years. Kickers and punters play for an average of 4.87 years.

(Go back to page 19.)

Playing Both Ways

Football players who play both offense and defense are known as "two-way" players. Before 1950, it was common for professional football players to play both offense and defense. However, in pro football's modern era—the years since 1950—very few two-way players have been successful.

Some players are such good athletes that coaches may be tempted to use them on both offense and defense. Defensive backs have the speed to keep up with wide receivers, so some people think they can also be good receivers. Tight ends and linebackers have similar physical gifts. Even many of today's mighty linemen have the agility and balance to use their size and power as **short-yardage backs**.

There are several reasons why two-way players remain uncommon in the NFL. One reason is that just playing one position well takes great dedication and focus. When a player tries to play two positions, his performance at one will probably suffer. Another reason is that playing two ways requires a huge physical effort. If a player is his team's defensive back on one play and its wide receiver on the next, he will not get a chance to rest. By the end of the game, he won't have the speed and energy needed to do both jobs. Finally, playing two positions increases a player's chance of injury. The risk may not be worth it. (Go back to page 22.) ◀◀

NFL Player Salaries

The National Football League has many rules about its players' salaries. All of the players in the league belong to the NFL Players Association, a union that helps make these rules. Some rules have to do with minimum salaries for players in the league. Other rules set the maximum that a team can spend on player salaries each season.

According to the rules, the least an NFL rookie can be paid is $285,000. As a player gains more experience, his minimum salary rises. For a player with 10 or more seasons in the league, the least a team can pay is $820,000.

Many NFL players are paid much more than the league minimum, of course. However, teams cannot pay players whatever they want because of the league's salary cap. The salary cap is the maximum amount a team is allowed to spend on player salaries. The reason for this rule is to help keep all of the teams competitive. If there was no salary cap, the richest teams could simply outspend the other teams and get all the top players.

Top NFL salaries—such as Champ Bailey's $63 million contract—sound huge. Players do not, however, automatically receive all that money. To get paid the full amount of a contract, a player has to play for a certain number of years and, often, achieve certain goals during each season.

(Go back to page 29.)

The Illegal Contact Rule

NFL rules say that defensive players are not allowed to touch or bump a receiver once that receiver is five yards beyond the line of scrimmage. The league's rule about illegal contact is sometimes called the "no chuck" rule. A *chuck* is the act by a defender of bumping a receiver while he is running his pass route. This is done to knock the receiver off balance and disrupt the timing between the receiver and the quarterback.

The no chuck rule was originally written in 1978. However, over the years the rule was not always enforced. During the 2003 playoffs, there were numerous examples of defensive backs who hung onto receivers so that they could not catch long passes. After this, the National Football League announced that its on-field officials would enforce the rules more strictly beginning in the 2004 season.

Stricter enforcement of the no chuck rule helps NFL offenses by making it easier for wide receivers to get open. Some people think rules like this are made to encourage more of the big plays that fans like to see. What helps the players on offense makes the game harder for defenders—particularly the cornerbacks who cover wide receivers. Now that defensive players are not allowed to make contact with the wide receivers they cover, they have had to learn to cover their opponents better. The defenders must be able to stay with the receivers, and place themselves in a good position to knock down or intercept passes.

Because Champ was already an outstanding cover cornerback, tighter enforcement of the rules did not have much of an effect on the way he played. Still, he was critical of the change. In 2004, he told *Sports Illustrated*:

> **❝**I've learned that as long as you're on defense, you'll never get a helping hand from the NFL. That's why cornerbacks need to be the highest-paid players in the league.**❞**

Because Champ also plays wide receiver on occasion, *Sports Illustrated* reporter Jeffri Chadiha asked whether he felt the rule helped him on offense. Champ said,

> **❝**The rules should be the same for everybody—offensive players shouldn't be able to touch defensive players either. There are only so many cornerbacks out there who can cover receivers with the rules in place. That helps me out as far as the money to be made, because I'm one of those players.**❞**

(Go back to page 30.)

No More Sideline "Force-outs"

Before the 2008 season, the National Football League made several changes to the rules of the pro game. One of these was to eliminate a rule regarding catches that occur near the sidelines. In professional football, a receiver must land both feet in bounds for the catch to count. However, in previous seasons, if a receiver was pushed while in the air making the catch, and landed out of bounds, the referee would have to make a judgment call. If the referee decided that the receiver would have landed in bounds had he not been pushed, the referee could rule that the pass had been completed successfully.

Beginning in 2008, NFL officials can no longer rule that a player was "forced out" on catches along the sidelines. All that matters is whether the receiver's feet both land inbounds when he makes a catch.

The purpose of this rule change is to make ruling on plays at the sidelines more consistent from one game to another. Opinions about whether a catch could have been made inbounds may differ from one referee to the next. These opinions no longer have a role in the calls that the referees make.

Some football commentators see this rule change as favoring the defense. If a cornerback is guarding a receiver near the sideline, all the cornerback has to do to keep the receiver's catch from counting is to make sure the receiver is out of bounds before he can get both feet on the ground.

The rule also applies to defensive players making interceptions, however. For an interception to count, the defensive player must have both feet on the ground inbounds when he intercepts the pass.

Although this rule takes away the referees' power to make "force-out" calls, it also makes their jobs a lot easier on what has always been a rather tough call. They no longer have to make split-second calls based only on their "feeling," or judgment, as to whether a player might or might not have caught a pass had he not been "forced out" of bounds.

(Go back to page 42.)

Brothers in the NFL

Very few people are able to become professional football players. Not many people have the skills and qualities that pro football requires. NFL players are not just big men. They are also fast and well coordinated. Even the best college football players have to make adjustments and improve in order to succeed in the NFL.

Size and athletic ability are characteristics that can be passed down genetically from parents to children. As a result, families that have one NFL player sometimes have another one—or even two. In the history of the NFL, there have been over 300 pairs of brothers who have played in the league.

Among the most famous NFL brothers today are Payton and Eli Manning. Both of the Manning brothers are among the best quarterbacks in the league. Their father, Archie Manning, was an NFL quarterback himself in the 1970s. Other pairs of brothers who are either currently playing or who played in recent years include Shannon and Sterling Sharpe, Carson and Jordan Palmer, Tiki and Ronde Barber, and Champ and Boss Bailey.

Although it is relatively unusual for two brothers to make it into the NFL, there have been 19 families from which three brothers played in the league. There are two families from which four brothers played in the NFL.

(Go back to page 42.) ◄◄

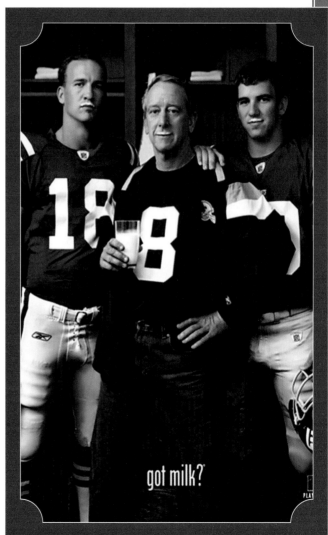

The Manning brothers Peyton (left) and Eli (right) pose with their father, Archie, for a "Got Milk?" ad. Both of the Manning brothers have won a Super Bowl (Peyton in 2007; Eli in 2008).

1978   Champ Bailey is born on June 22 in Folkston, Georgia.

1994   Plays quarterback and free safety for the football team at Charlton County High School. He also stars on the basketball and track teams.

1995   After moving to the tailback position, rushes for 1,858 yards and scores 28 touchdowns, leading his team to an 11–1 record and becoming the top high school recruit in the state.

1996   Begins attending the University of Georgia and makes the football team.

1998   Named defensive MVP of the Peach Bowl. After three seasons with the Bulldogs, he is considered one of the best college players in the country.

1999   Champ enters the NFL draft and is selected by the Washington Redskins with the seventh pick in the first round. Helps the Redskins win 10 games and earn a playoff spot.

2000   After a strong season, invited to participate in the Pro Bowl for the first time.

2001   Selected for his second Pro Bowl.

2002   In May, marries Hanady Aboneeaj. After another strong season, selected to the Pro Bowl again.

2003   The Redskins finish with a 5–11 record, but Champ is again recognized as a Pro Bowl player.

2004   When the Redskins and Champ cannot agree on a contract, Champ is traded to the Denver Broncos. Champ signs a seven-year, $63 million deal that makes him the highest-paid cornerback in NFL history. Has a good season for the Broncos and is selected for his fifth Pro Bowl.

2005   Champ helps the Broncos to a 13–3 regular-season record; is selected to the Pro Bowl for the sixth time.

2006   Finishes tied for the NFL lead in interceptions, with 10. Finishes second in the voting for NFL Defensive Player of the Year, and is selected to the Pro Bowl for the seventh time.

2007   Selected to the Pro Bowl for the eighth time.

2008   The Broncos sign Boss Bailey, Champ's younger brother, to a contract.

1995 Georgia Class-A high jump champion
All-state honorable mention in basketball

1996 Class-A All-State selection in football
USA Today honorable mention (football)
Second team All-South selection (football)

1998 Peach Bowl defensive MVP
Bronko Nagurski Award
All-America first team
All-SEC first-team selection.

1999 NFL Defensive Player of the Month for October

2000 Pro Bowl
Pro Football Weekly first team all-conference
Associated Press all-NFL (All-Pro) second team

2001 Pro Bowl

2002 Pro Bowl

2003 Pro Bowl
Pro Football Weekly first team all-conference
Associated Press second team all-NFL
Sporting News first team all-NFL

2004 Pro Bowl
Pro Football Weekly first team all-conference
Associated Press first team all-NFL
Pro Football Writers first team all-NFL
Sporting News first team all-NFL

2005 Pro Bowl
Pro Football Weekly first team all-conference
Associated Press first team all-NFL
Pro Football Writers first team all-NFL
Sporting News first team all-NFL

2006 Pro Bowl
Associated Press first team all-NFL

2007 Pro Bowl
Associated Press second team all-NFL

Career Statistics

Year	Team	G	Tot	Solo	Ast	PD	Sack	FF	FR	Int	Yds	TD
1999	WAS	16	79	73	6	17	1.0	2	0	5	55	1
2000	WAS	16	62	59	3	14	0.0	0	0	5	48	0
2001	WAS	16	51	49	2	18	0.0	1	0	3	17	0
2002	WAS	16	68	65	3	24	0.0	0	0	3	2	0
2003	WAS	16	72	69	3	9	0.0	1	0	2	2	0
2004	DEN	16	81	72	9	12	0.0	0	0	3	0	0
2005	DEN	14	66	60	6	23	0.0	1	0	8	139	2
2006	DEN	16	86	74	12	21	0.0	0	4	10	162	1
2007	DEN	15	84	71	13	14	0.0	0	0	3	3	0
Career		141	649	592	57	152	1.0	5	0	42	428	4

G = games
Tot = total tackles
Solo = solo tackles
Ast = assisted tackles
PD = passes defended
Sack = sacks recorded
FF = forced fumbles
FR = fumbles recovered
Int = interceptions
Yds = yards gained after interception
TD = touchdowns scored

Books and Periodicals

Dater, Adrian. *The Good, the Bad, and the Ugly Denver Broncos: Heart-Pounding, Jaw-Dropping, and Gut-Wrenching Moments in Broncos History*. Chicago: Triumph Books, 2007.

Gramling, Gary. "Mr. Shut Down." *Sports Illustrated for Kids* (December 3, 2007): p. 21.

Pompei, Dan. "Overrated? Not Bailey." *Sporting News* (August 26, 2005): p. 50–51.

Stewart, Mark. *The Denver Broncos*. Chicago: Norwood House, 2006.

Web Sites

www.champbailey.com

At Champ Bailey's official Web site, you can get updated information on Champ's statistics, results of Broncos games, photos of Champ, and information about the Bailey brothers' football camp.

www.denverbroncos.com

The Broncos' official team site includes video clips of big plays, team news, player statistics, and profiles of the team's stars.

www.nfl.com

The official site of the National Football League has information about the Denver Broncos and all the other teams in the league.

http://sports.espn.go.com/nfl/players/profile?playerId=1758

This Champ Bailey site managed by ESPN includes statistics and links to recent news articles.

www.georgiadogs.com

The official athletic site of the University of Georgia provides information about the Georgia Bulldogs football team.

agent—a businessperson whose job it is to represent an athlete or other client in contract negotiations.

breaks—sudden shifts in the direction or the speed of a receiver while running a pass route, in an attempt to create space between the receiver and the defender.

cornerback—a defensive player on a football team who usually plays farthest back from the line of scrimmage and who guards against deep pass plays by the offensive players.

curls—curving moves in a receiver's pass pattern, or route, done in an attempt to create space between him and the defender.

cuts—sharp moves in a receiver's pass pattern.

draft—in sports, the annual process by which teams select new players from the college or amateur ranks, with teams that performed poorly during the past season picking before those with better records.

free safety—a defensive football player who does not guard a specific opponent, instead playing defense wherever needed.

fumble—in football, the loss of the ball by a player as a result of it being dropped or knocked out of his hands.

interception—when a pass intended for an offensive player (one of the receivers) is caught instead by one of the defensive players, giving possession to the defense.

out routes—pass patterns for a receiver that feature a cut or a curl from the inside part of the football field toward the sideline.

Pro Bowl—the NFL all-star game between the American Football Conference (AFC) and the National Football Conference (NFC), played by those players chosen to be the best at their position.

quadriceps—the large muscle of the upper leg.

quarterback—the player on a football team who tells the team what play they are running and moves the ball to a running back or receiver after the snap.

sack—to tackle a quarterback before he can pass the ball.

short-yardage back—an offensive player who specializes in carrying the ball short distances.

tailback—in football, the player who takes the position behind the quarterback and, after the play begins, is most likely to carry the ball.

touchdown—in football, the carrying or catching of the ball beyond the opponent's goal line, resulting in a score that is worth six points.

wide receiver—a receiver who typically lines up farthest away from the center and who usually runs the deeper pass routes

page 7 "Big-time players . . ." Jeff Legwold, "Bailey Making Foes Pay for Tossing Ball His Way," *Rocky Mountain News* (January 19, 2006). http://www.rockymountainnews.com/news/2006/jan/19/bailey-making-foes-pay-for-tossing-ball-his-way

page 7 "[Quarterback Tom Brady] . . ." Legwold, "Bailey Making Foes Pay for Tossing Ball His Way."

page 9 "[Champ is] just cat-quick . . ." Matt Pitzer, "Bailey, Polamalu second to none in secondary," *USA Today* (June 17, 2006), p. C3.

page 11 "[Champ] was so active . . ." Mike Klis, "Divided Loyalties End for Baileys," *Denver Post* (March 8, 2008). http://www.denverpost.com/ci_8508134?source=rss

page 11 "the neighborhood girl athlete" Klis, "Divided Loyalties End for Baileys."

page 12 "I tried to take care . . ." Frank Schwab, "Bronco's Bailey Forced to Grow up Fast," *Colorado Springs Gazette* (September 20, 2004). http://www.gazette.com/onset?id=159&template=article.html

page 15 "From the minute he stepped . . ." Michael Bradley, "2 for 1," *The Sporting News* (March 8, 1999). http://findarticles.com/p/articles/mi_m1208/is_10_223/ai_54117606

page 18 "I was anxious to meet . . ." Dennis Tuttle, "In Champ's Corner," *The Sporting News* (October 11, 1999).

page 19 "Coming out of college . . ." Tuttle, "In Champ's Corner."

page 19 "Just one month . . ." Tuttle, "In Champ's Corner."

page 21 "What I'm proud of . . ." Tuttle, "In Champ's Corner."

page 25 "Now I know . . ." Mark Maske, "Amid Farewell, Welcome Relief," *Washington Post* (December 30, 2002). http://www.washingtonpost.com/wp-dyn/articles/A50755-2002Dec29.html

page 29 "A happy medium ultimately . . ." Lee Rasizer, "Win-Windfall Situation All Around," *Rocky Mountain News* (March 5, 2004).

page 29 "I can promise one thing . . ." Andrew Mason, "Bailey Becomes the Newest Bronco," denverbroncos.com (March 4, 2004). http://www.denverbroncos.com/page.php?id=334&storyID=2061

page 30 "I think Champ's really ecstatic . . ." "Bailey Gets $63 Million Deal from Broncos," Associated Press (March 5, 2004). http://nbcsports.msnbc.com/id/4442099/

page 30 "I think both teams got . . ." Jon Robinson, "Champ Bailey Interview," *IGN* (November 23, 2004). http://sports.ign.com/articles/568/568506p1.html

page 32 "Champ Bailey has not only . . ." Robinson, "Champ Bailey Interview"

page 33 "It's definitely more challenging . . ." Quoted in Jeffri Chadiha, "Champ Bailey: Broncos Cornerback," *Sports Illustrated* (November 22, 2004), p. 37

page 36 "I think you kind of feed . . ." Jon Robinson, "Champ Bailey: First and Ten," *IGN* (January 20, 2006). http://sports.ign.com/articles/682/682419p1.html

page 39 "That's why you throw . . ." "Manning-to-Wayne helps unbeaten Colts burn Broncos," Associated Press (October 29, 2006). http://sports-att.espn.go.com/nfl/recap?gameId=261029007

page 40 "Champ's a guy that works . . ." Arnie Stapleton, "Can Bailey Do Any Better Than Last Year?" Associated Press (May 21, 2007). http://www.usatoday.com/sports/football/2007-05-21-1996605401_x.htm

page 41 "He's the most complete . . ." Gary Gramling, "Mr. Shut Down," *Sports Illustrated for Kids* (December 3, 2007).

page 42 "It's a little bittersweet . . . ." Press Release, "Champ Bailey Named Pro Bowl Starter," Scout.com (December 18, 2007). http://den.scout.com/2/712736.html

page 42 "[Boss] brings athleticism . . . ." "Champ Bailey Says He'll Take Marshall under His Wing," Associated Press (March 25, 2008). http://sports.espn.go.com/espn/wire?section=nfl&id=3312082

page 45 "He sees everything . . . ." Gramling, "Mr. Shut Down."

page 45 "I don't go out . . . ." Pitzer, "Bailey, Polamalu Second to None in Secondary."

page 45 "Champ Bailey simply, consistently . . ." Jeff Legwold, "Team Returns to Laboratory," *Rocky Mountain News* (January 1, 2008). http://www.rockymountainnews.com/news/2008/jan/01/legwold-offseason-tweaking-ready-begin/

page 52 "I've learned that as long . . ." Quoted in Chadiha, "Champ Bailey: Broncos Cornerback," *Sports Illustrated*, p. 37

page 52 "The rules should be . . ." Quoted in Chadiha, "Champ Bailey: Broncos Cornerback," *Sports Illustrated*, p. 37

Numbers in **bold italics** refer to captions.

D. C. Snow has worked as a professional writer for over 30 years, developing training materials, marketing and advertising programs, internal communications vehicles, public relations campaigns, and audiovisual scripts for dozens of clients, including IBM, the U.S. Navy, McGraw-Hill Publishing, and AT&T. Snow holds a master's degree in the teaching of writing and has taught writing, marketing, and public relations courses at the university and postgraduate levels. He and his wife reside in Charlotte, North Carolina.

PICTURE CREDITS

page

5: Denver Broncos/SPCS
6: Matthew Emmons/US Presswire/Zuma
8: William R. Amatucci Sr./NFL/WireImage
11: Denver Post/PRMS
13: Jennifer Pack/T&T/IOA Photos
14: Pacific Paramount/NMI
17: Upper Deck/NMI
18: George Bridges/KRT
20: SportsChrome Pix
23: George Bridges/KRT
24: TV Guide/NMI
27: SportsChrome Pix
28: Jim Prisching/Chicago Tribune/KRT

31: Jerilee Bennett/Colorado Springs Gazette/KRT
32: Mark Cornelison/Lexington Herald-Leader/KRT
34: Mark Reis/Colorado Springs Gazette/KRT
37: Jeffery Beall/SPCS
38: Mike Ehrmann/WireImage
41: Charlie Lyons Pardue/SPCS
43: Kevin C. Cox/Getty Images
44: IOS Photos
46: Bernard Gagnon/SPCS
49: Dave Akins/SPCS
50: NFL/Photo File/SPCS
54: Milk PEP/NMI

Front cover: Mike Ehrmann/WireImage
Front cover inset: Denver Post/PRMS